AF270439

LONDON'S SWINGIN' 60S & 70S

First published in the UK in 2022 by Supernova Books, an imprint of Aurora Metro Publications Ltd.
80 Hill Rise, Richmond, TW10 6UB UK
www.aurorametro.com info@aurorametro.com
Twitter: @aurorametro F: facebook.com/AuroraMetroBooks
Pop Rock Icons; London's Swingin' 60s and 70s

Printed by Short Run Press, Exeter, UK on sustainably resourced paper.
ISBNs:
978-1-913641-26-9 (print)
978-1-913641-27-6 (ebook)

LONDON'S SWINGIN' 60S & 70S

BY
PHILIPPE MARGOTIN
TRANSLATED BY CHERYL ROBSON

WITH A FOREWORD BY
DAVID SINCLAIR

ABOUT THE AUTHORS

PHILIPPE MARGOTIN

Musical adviser for *Le Petit Larousse* (French dictionary), editor in chief for Universal Group (*Rhythm'n'blues*, *Blues Story*, *Rock Story*, and TV series like *The Avengers*, *Columbo*, *Murder She Wrote*, *Miami Vice*, Margotin, has devoted himself for many years to rock music and its universe. He's the co-writer of the *All The Songs* Collection (Black Dog/Leventhal) and the series *Beatles*, *Dylan*, *Rolling Stones*, *Pink Floyd*, *Led Zeppelin*, *Hendrix*, *Springsteen* (Octopus). This series, which has been translated into English, German, Spanish, Italian, Dutch, Chinese (for Dylan!), exceeded 600,000 copies sold around the world.

Recent books include: *Open the Doors* and *Highway To Hell: AC/DC* (Glenat); *The Universe of the Beatles* and *The Universe of The Clash* (La Martinière). He's also the creator and the editor in chief of *Planet Metal* Collection published by Hachette. In 2020, he wrote the radio program *Get Back — the Sound of the Beatles*.

DAVID SINCLAIR

Sinclair has been a musician since the 70s and a music journalist since the 80s. As chief rock/pop correspondent of *The Times* of London and a contributor to *Rolling Stone*, *Billboard*, *Q* magazine and many others, he was fortunate to see and meet many of the bands and stars who came up through the London gig circuit. He is a contributor to *Rock's Diamond Year* also for Supernova Books about the London club scene.

As a singer, songwriter and bandleader of David Sinclair Four (DS4), Sinclair has been privileged to have played at many of the London clubs and music venues himself. www.davidsinclairfour.com

Supergroup Emerson, Lake and Palmer (ELP) performing *Tarkus* on stage

CONTENTS

01.

FOREWORD
BY DAVID SINCLAIR

WHAT PEOPLE FORGET ABOUT POP MUSIC IN THE UK AT THE START OF THE 1960S WAS THE EXTRAORDINARY EFFORT YOU HAD TO MAKE TO HEAR IT. YOU MIGHT STUMBLE UPON A CHUCK BERRY TRACK ON THE BBC KIDS' RADIO PROGRAMME *Saturday Club* OR CATCH A GLIMPSE OF THE SEARCHERS ON THE ONLY TV MUSIC SHOW *Thank Your Lucky Stars*. OTHERWISE, IT WAS A CASE OF TUNING INTO RADIO LUXEMBOURG, WHERE THE SONGS WERE DELIBERATELY FADED BY THE DJ BEFORE THE END. IF YOU MANAGED TO HEAR A SONG YOU LIKED, YOU HAD TO DASH OUT AND BUY THE RECORD TO BE SURE OF EVER HEARING IT AGAIN.

THE ARRIVAL OF THE BEATLES AND THE ROLLING STONES INTO THIS WORLD OF RESTRICTED BROADCASTING AND GREY CULTURAL CONFORMITY TRIGGERED A BIG BANG THAT ECHOES TO THIS DAY. THESE TWO GROUPS BROUGHT A NEW SOUND AND IMAGE TO THE TABLE WHICH PROMPTED A WORLDWIDE MUSICAL AND SOCIAL REVOLUTION. HERE, PHILIPPE MARGOTIN HAS ASSEMBLED A MAGICAL PARADE OF PHOTOGRAPHS WHICH CAPTURES THE SPIRIT OF A TIME WHEN FASHION, CULTURE AND THE ARTS WERE DRIVEN BY THE BRITISH MUSIC AND MUSICIANS OF THE 1960S AND 1970S.

As a schoolboy in London, the great awakening began for me with the arrival of pirate radio in 1964. Suddenly, you could tune in to Radio Caroline or Big L (aka Wonderful Radio London) and hear new records by the Kinks, the Animals, the Yardbirds, the Move, Manfred Mann, and the Who along with American hits by the Byrds, the Lovin' Spoonful, Bob Dylan and many others.

As the sun rose on the summer of love in 1967, the clash of cultures and the sense of a changing of the guard between generations was palpable. I bought a kaftan and started my own group. We learned to play songs by Jimi Hendrix and Cream almost as soon as they were released, and mastered Love Sculpture's epic version of Aram Kachaturian's *Sabre Dance*. I saw Free at the Fairfield Halls in Croydon supported by the English "renaissance folk" band Amazing Blondel, whose music harked back to the 12th century court of King Richard I.

In 1969, our music teacher at school took us to see Deep Purple performing with the Royal Philharmonic Orchestra at the Albert Hall where they recorded Jon Lord's *Concerto for Group and Orchestra*. I saw Hendrix for the third and final time at the Isle of Wight Festival in 1970, an event which put the UK music scene on the front pages of newspapers and magazines around the world.

I gawped at David Bowie's entrance in *Starman* mode on *Top of The Pops* in 1972, and later discovered that everyone else had done exactly the same. The glam-rock style was embraced by groups as different as Roxy Music and Mott the Hoople and by emerging stars from Elton John to Rod Stewart. I bought a pair of platform boots. Agony! And in 1975 I went to see Queen in their pomp at Hammersmith Odeon with costumes by Zandra Rhodes.

They took it all too far...but away from the glitz and the increasingly remote spectacle of the international arena-rock circuit which Pink Floyd, Led Zeppelin and the Stones were now establishing, I started hanging out at the Nashville Pub in North End Road and the Hope & Anchor in Islington, where a new generation of pub-rock groups such as Dr. Feelgood, Ian Dury and the Blockheads and the Stranglers were taking rock & roll back to basics.

Nowadays, music is everywhere. You can download virtually any song you want to hear at almost any time from just about anywhere on the planet. It is part of the cultural air that we all breathe. Yet with so much to choose from, the catalogues of the stars which started their journey from these islands in the 1960s and 1970s remain the gold standard by which contemporary pop and rock music is still judged. Their stories and images remain a source of wonder and celebration of a time when young people were inspired to change the world. For those too young to remember the spirit and energy of those decades, this book offers a glimpse of that world in the pages that follow.

02.

INTRODUCTION
BY PHILIPPE MARGOTIN

"A LOT OF PEOPLE SEEM TO THINK I STARTED
THIS BUSINESS. BUT ROCK 'N' ROLL WAS HERE
A LONG TIME BEFORE I CAME ALONG. NOBODY
CAN SING THAT KIND OF MUSIC LIKE COLORED
PEOPLE. LET'S FACE IT: I CAN'T SING LIKE FATS
DOMINO CAN. I KNOW THAT."

– ELVIS PRESLEY

The musical revolution in the land of Her Majesty the Queen's Britannia took place just a few years after the emergence in the United States of a teenage culture that went by the name of rock'n'roll. It was in Liverpool that the fuse was lit. The chief arsonists of the blaze were John Lennon, Paul McCartney, George Harrison and Ringo Starr. Gathered under the name of The Beatles, they created their first few brilliant melodies – 'Please Please Me', 'From Me to You', 'She Loves You', 'I Want To Hold Your Hand' – and, suddenly, the whole country was on fire, seduced by their catchy Mersey beat.

In London, the Rolling Stones were taking matters into their own hands. Mick Jagger, Brian Jones, Keith Richards, Bill Wyman and Charlie Watts played the blues as if their lives depended on it and, under the aegis of their manager Andrew Loog Oldham, they came to symbolise the darker side of Liverpool's Fab Four.

First The Beatles and the Rolling Stones, then the Yardbirds, Them, The Who, the Kinks, the Spencer Davis Group, the Animals... English rock? It became a tidal wave of new music, which by the mid-1960s, swept across Europe and the United States and became known as the "British Invasion".

"I used to think anyone doing anything weird was weird. Now I know that it is the people that call others weird that are weird."

— PAUL MCCARTNEY

This British supremacy in music would continue for two decades and diverge into multiple exciting currents. After the Mersey sound of The Beatles and the driving rhythm 'n' blues of the Rolling Stones, an explosion of pop and mod music emerged from Dusty Springfield to Donovan, through The Who, Procol Harum, to the Troggs. Unstoppable, this exciting force of musical energy and ideas flowed into the progressive rock music of bands like Pink Floyd, Yes, and Genesis.

Later, as the drugs took hold and the Vietnam War got under way, the heavy metal of Led Zeppelin, Black Sabbath and Deep Purple reflected darker moods, while the glam rock of T. Rex, Roxy Music and David Bowie rode on a new wave of gender fluidity.

It would be hard to describe the immense creativity of the times without mentioning the mastery and experimentation of guitar heroes such as Eric Clapton, Jeff Beck, and Ritchie Blackmore – not to mention the legendary Jimi Hendrix who, although an American, had risen to the top, thanks to his popularity with the British public.

Due to the current wave of renewed interest in the prodigious English music scene of the 1960s and 1970s, driven in part by younger generations discovering these bands on YouTube and Spotify for the first time, this book revisits the era for a new audience. For those who are long-time fans, the photographs in this book offer a reminder of the age and a glimpse behind the scenes.

Taken by some of the best photographers, the images which have been carefully collected in this book not only celebrate the era but they capture the spirit of this incredible countercultural movement.

Twenty years of freedom and creativity that changed the world!

STONES VERSUS BEATLES

03.

STONES VERSUS BEATLES

"THEY LOOK LIKE BOYS WHOM ANY SELF-RESPECTING MUM WOULD LOCK IN THE BATHROOM. BUT THE ROLLING STONES, FIVE TOUGH YOUNG LONDON-BASED MUSIC MAKERS WITH DOORSTEP MOUTHS, PALLID CHEEKS AND UNKEMPT HAIR ARE NOT WORRIED WHAT MUMS THINK!"

– JUDITH SIMONS

These few lines are taken from the *Daily Express*, the day after the concert that the Rolling Stones gave in Cardiff on February 28, 1964.

Double previous page: Brian Jones, Mick Jagger, Keith Richards, Charlie Watts and Bill Wyman with journalist Thomas Beyl in London in 1966. Smirking, pouting, a little disillusioned…, the Stones liked to act provocatively in front of the camera.

Although the piece was written by journalist Judith Simons, somehow it bears the stamp of Andrew Loog Oldham. He had stepped in to replace Giorgio Gomelsky as the manager of the Stones after seeing them at the Crawdaddy Club in Richmond on April 21, 1963, while Gomelsky was abroad for a funeral. Oldham set about finding them a recording contract (signed with Decca in May 1963) and knew his main priority was – above all – to shape their image.

Having been Brian Epstein's assistant at NEMS (North End Music Stores), which managed the career of the Beatles, and with a good understanding of how the media worked, he had the idea of making the London Five the dark, subversive version of the Liverpool Four. Working in partnership with newspapers, television, and radio, he began to transform Mick Jagger, Brian Jones, Keith Richards, Bill Wyman and Charlie Watts into the bad boys of the British music scene.

"Would you let your sister go out with a Rolling Stone?" asked *Melody Maker* on March 14, 1964. Oldham hit the nail on the head when he wrote on the band's debut album: "The Rolling Stones are more than a band. They are a way of life."

As for the scandals that would punctuate the entire second half of the 1960s – linked to the band's illicit consumption of drugs and misogynistic statements – they were all cleverly devised to keep the flame burning.

Everything that was orchestrated by Oldham was intended to distinguish the Rolling Stones from the Beatles. While the Beatles were performing with smiles, dressed in suits, with neatly combed hairstyles, the Stones loved to dress in velvet or leather, wear their hair long and scruffy, at the same time as cultivating a disillusioned sneer.

Musically, too, the difference was striking. While Lennon and McCartney composed beautiful upbeat melodies, which captured the zeitgeist, Jagger and Richards drew inspiration from the African-American blues anthems which they covered before being forced to write their own repertoire. One example of this difference is the Beatles singing 'I Want to Hold Your Hand', while the Rolling Stones were far more explicit, singing 'I Just Want to Make Love to You' in their cover of Willie Dixon's song.

Even though the Beatles and the Rolling Stones were obvious competitors in public, they nevertheless remained friends in private. A few years after recording Lennon-McCartney's 'I Wanna Be Your Man' for their second single (1963), Mick Jagger and Keith Richards would happily sing on the chorus of the recording of 'All You Need Is Love' (1967) by the Beatles.

Left page: British tradition obliges! John Lennon, Ringo Starr, George Harrison and Paul McCartney take a golf lesson. "Help! I need somebody," the Beatles sing...
Above: George Harrison, the most romantic of the Beatles, with his girlfriend Pattie Boyd. The happy encounter took place in 1964, during the filming of Richard Lester's film *A Hard Day's Night*.

Above: Brian Jones, the founder and blond guitarist of the Rolling Stones, and Anita Pallenberg
were one of the most glamorous couples of the sixties. Anita first saw Brian at a concert in
September 1965. Love at first sight. "Next to him, Mick and Keith were little schoolchildren,"
she recalled.
Right page: the London Five in 1965. The Rolling Stones also submit to a round of golf.
The greens are clearly not their cup of tea.

Left page: Decorated by the Queen on October 26, 1965, The Beatles proudly displa
their Member of the British Empire medals. The honour testifies to the popularity
the influence, but also the economic weight of the Fab Four
Above: The Stones in Bremen, Federal Germany, May 29, 1967. They may not have
been received at Buckingham Palace, but the gold records are raining down

“We're more popular than Jesus now; I don't know which will go first – rock 'n' roll or Christianity.”

– JOHN LENNON

Double previous page: Michael Philip Jagger in the early 1970s.
Profession: singer of the Rolling Stones. Claim to fame: number one
sex symbol of the rock'n'roll scene.
Above: John Lennon photographed in 1967. An exceptional year for The Beatles
who released the single 'Strawberry Fields Forever/Penny Lane' and the masterful
album *Sgt. Pepper's Lonely Hearts Club Band*. John was at the zenith of his art with
'Strawberry Fields Forever', which is an evocation of the Liverpool of his childhood,
but also with 'Lucy in the Sky With Diamonds', shortened to "LSD" chiming with
the Summer of Love.

Double previous page: John, George, Paul and Ringo in 1969. The Beatles' separation is
near. "The end of the dream", one might say...
Above: In a fetching black hat, and spectacles, Keith Richards, in 1967, has a rare talent
for cultivating the art of derision. He played the judge in the video of 'For We Love You',
which was a Stones-style interpretation of Oscar Wilde's trial in 1895. Mick Jagger
played Oscar Wilde, the Irish writer, and Marianne Faithfull his boyfriend, Lord Alfred
Douglas.

John Lennon during the filming of *Magical Mystery Tour*, the 1967 television film directed by Bernard Knowles for the BBC. The idea: the four Beatles go on a trip aboard a bus that will cross the English countryside. The beginning of a long series of burlesque gags punctuated by some of the Beatles' most beautiful songs, such as 'I Am The Walrus' and 'The Fool On The Hill'.
Next double page: Group portrait during the Rock and Roll Circus organized by the Stones in December 1968. From right to left: Brian Jones, Yoko Ono, Roger Daltrey (the singer of The Who), the young Julian Lennon and John.

'N' BLUES

04.

RHYTHM'N'BLUES

IN THE EARLY 1960S, BLUES FROM THE MISSISSIPPI DELTA AND SMOKY CHICAGO CLUBS SYMBOLIZED THE MUSIC OF THE FUTURE FOR A YOUNG GENERATION OF ENGLISH TEENAGERS.

THE TRUE ORIGINS OF THE ENGLISH RHYTHM'N'BLUES REVOLUTION BEGAN WITH THE LIKES OF ALEXIS KORNER AND CYRIL DAVIES. KORNER'S BLUES INCORPORATED, PLAYING IN THE DAMP BASEMENT OF THE EALING CLUB, FOR EXAMPLE, INCLUDED MICK JAGGER, KEITH RICHARDS AND CHARLIE WATTS (FUTURE ROLLING STONES), GINGER BAKER AND JACK BRUCE (FUTURE CREAM), ERIC BURDON (FUTURE SINGER OF THE ANIMALS), WHILE PIANIST NICKY HOPKINS AND SINGER LONG JOHN BALDRY WERE MEMBERS OF THE CYRIL DAVIES ALL-STARS, ONE OF THE FIRST BANDS TO INCLUDE A TRIO OF BLACK FEMALE BACKING SINGERS KNOWN AS THE VELVETTES.

Double previous page: Rod Stewart, one of the most distinctive voices of English rhythm'n'blues, alongside Paul McCartney and his wife, Linda.

If the Rolling Stones came to be the most well-known exponents of English rhythm'n'blues, other individuals and groups would also play their part in this musical revolution. This is particularly true of John Mayall, who in 1962, set up the band Bluesbreakers. Four years later, with a young guitar prodigy named Eric Clapton, the Bluesbreakers recorded their first masterpiece, the aptly named album, *Blues Breakers* with Eric Clapton. Joe Cocker, who made his studio debut in 1964 recording a cover of The Beatles' 'I'll Cry Instead', also established himself from 1967 as one of the seminal voices of English R'n'B with another Beatles cover, 'With a Little Help from My Friends'.

The Yardbirds are among the few bands capable of comparison with the Rolling Stones. Incredibly, the Yardbirds would include in various line-ups, three of the biggest guitar heroes in rock history, namely Eric Clapton, Jeff Beck and Jimmy Page.

Among the other bands of the British R'n'B scene, singer Eric Burdon and The Animals would occupy a special place, due to the influence of traditional African-American folk songs, notably in their unforgettable reinterpretation in 1964 of the 'House Of The Rising Sun' with Burdon's soulful vocals and Alan Price's moving gospel organ accompaniment.

Two influential bands which are now being rediscovered, namely Them and the Pretty Things, remained very close to the tradition of the electric blues while Manfred Mann found a path to success by combining rhythm'n'blues with jazz and pop. A special mention, also, to the Spencer Davis Group, which acted as a springboard to glory for singer and multi-instrumentalist Steve Winwood.

In the wake of the Stones and the Yardbirds, dozens of bands across the UK were converted to the language of the blues. Critics even spoke of a "blues boom", a phenomenon that reached its zenith at the National Jazz and Blues Festival, which had had its beginnings a few years earlier in Richmond, but moved to Windsor in the glorious summer of 1967. The weekend festival included Fleetwood Mac, consisting of ex-Bluesbreakers Mick Fleetwood (drums), Peter Green (guitar) and John McVie (bass), who were joined by Jeremy Spencer (vocals, guitar). Chicken Shack, too, was warmly applauded in Windsor, with singer Christine Perfect (John McVie's future wife), guitarist Stan Webb, bassist Sylvester and drummer Dave Bidwell, supported by a red-hot brass section, establishing itself as one of the very best interpreters of the English blues.

Other bands which emerged during this second blues boom include Savoy Brown (one of the earliest multi-cultural bands), Ten Years After and Jethro Tull (before they made a spectacular turn towards progressive rock).

The members of Them at the Ruislip Lido (near London) in 1967. We recognize
the singer Van Morrison (the second from the right). After the phenomenal
success of 'Gloria' in 1964, the Belfast-born band also became a regular on the
London scene. The key to their success: a fiery reinterpretation of the electric
blues, that of John Lee Hooker, Muddy Waters and Jimmy Reed.

Top: Manfred Mann in 1966 with vocalist Mike D'Abo (left) as
Paul Jones' successor and bassist Klaus Voorman (right).
Above: In 1965, the English rhythm'n'blues band included
(from left to right) Manfred Mann, Paul Jones, Tom
McGuinness and Mike Hugg. Its consecration came the
previous year when the song '5-4-3-2-1' was chosen as the
theme song of the show *Ready Steady Go!*
Next double page: Manfred Mann in 1968.

ALEXIS KORNER

Alexis Korner and bassist Jack Bruce. Guitarist and singer Alexis Korner was
one of the very first to introduce the blues to audiences in the United Kingdom
in the early 1960s. His band, Blues Incorporated, was a real laboratory where
the talents of Mick Jagger and Charlie Watts, the future Rolling Stones, and
also Jack Bruce and Ginger Baker of the future Cream, hatched.

Long John Baldry is another key figure in the English rhythm'n'blues of the 1960s. After singing with Alexis Korner's Blues Incorporated, he took over the reins of Cyril Davies and his Rhythm and Blues All Stars upon Davies' death (1964), a band he renamed Long John Baldry and his Hoochie Coochie Men. At his side was a young singer from the London borough of Highgate named Rod Stewart.

THE YARDBIRDS

The Yardbirds came out of the shadows when they succeeded the Rolling
Stones on the stage of the Crawdaddy Club in Richmond in 1963 with a
repertoire of old blues. Then they entered the annals of rock legend for
launching three guitar heroes: Eric Clapton, Jeff Beck and Jimmy Page.
Above: The Yardbirds' second line-up. From left to right: Chris Dreja, Keith
Relf, Jeff Beck, Jim McCarty and Paul Samwell-Smith.

The Animals made their debut in 1963. In June the following year, they reached number one on the UK charts with a rock reinterpretation of the traditional American blues number, 'House of the Rising Sun'. The key to their success: Alan Price's gospel organ and Eric Burdon's expressive, bluesy voice. Above, from left to right: John Steel, Eric Burdon, Chas Chandler, Hilton Valentine and Alan Price.

Left page: Stevie Winwood, a Ray Charles voice with a British distinction...
Top and above: The Spencer Davis Group blew a new wind on English rhythm'n'blues
with 'Gimme Some Lovin'', number 2 in the British charts in the autumn of 1966.
Next double page: Birmingham's line-up includes (from left to right) Stevie Winwood,
Muff Winwood, Peter York and Spencer Davis.

TRAFFIC

In 1967, Stevie Winwood (in the foreground) left the Spencer Davis Group for a new adventure at the head of Traffic. They added new sensibilities to rhythm'n'blues – psychedelic rock, folk, jazz – as evidenced by the albums *Mr Fantasy* (1967), *Traffic* (1968), then, after Mason's departure, *John Barleycorn Must Die* (1970). Above: Stevie Winwood in the foreground; from left to right: Chris Wood, Jim Capaldi and Dave Mason.

Julie Driscoll was the number one female singer of English R'n'B in the 1960s, as well as being a leading figure of style and fashion. In 1965, she sang in Steampacket with Rod Stewart (far left), Long John Baldry and Brian Auger (right). Two years later, she was the sublime voice of Brian Auger & Trinity. Their versions of Aretha Franklin's 'Save Me' and Bob Dylan and Rick Danko's 'This Wheel's On Fire' are unforgettable.

JOHN MAYALL

John Mayall is the archetypal ambassador of African-American blues in British lands. In 1963, he founded the Bluesbreakers, a springboard to fame for several generations of musicians, including guitarists Eric Clapton, Peter Green and Mick Taylor. Released in 1966, with Otis Rush's 'All Your Love' and Robert Johnson's 'Ramblin' On My Mind', *Blues Breakers With Eric Clapton* will go down as one of the most striking albums of British rhythm'n'blues.

Above: Fleetwood Mac early era. From left to right: Peter Green, John McVie,
Mike Fleetwood and Jeremy Spencer. Revealed at the National Jazz and Blues
Festival of 1967, the group emerges with its first album,
a manifesto of English rhythm'n'blues.
Next double page: In 1973, Fleetwood Mac included (from left to right) Bob
Weston, Christine McVie, Bob Welch, John McVie and Mick Fleetwood. And
records the excellent *Mystery to Me*.

"For me, the focus are songs which really get the audience moving."

– JOE COCKER

Joe Cocker's journey began in the mining town of Sheffield in the north of England. He would continue to take centre stage in rhythm'n'blues for several years, to the point of being one of the key players at Woodstock in August 1969. Then he sings 'With A Little Help From My Friends', to the flower power generation. There will be many more hits, sung in a hoarse voice. Joe Cocker is also a great stage performer.

ROD STEWART

In the 1960s, especially with Steampacket, there was no salvation for Rod Stewart outside of rhythm'n'blues. Subsequently, he broadened his style, but, whether in folk, rock'n'roll and even disco, the voice of the one who was understandably nicknamed "Rod The Mod" would remain immediately recognizable.
Next double page: The Faces. From left to right: Ian McLagan, Rod Stewart, Ronnie Wood, Kenney Jones and Tetsu Yamauchi.

05.

MODS & SWINGIN' LONDON

THE EXTRAORDINARY CREATIVE TURBULENCE THAT ENGLAND EXPERIENCED IN THE 1960S WAS FUELLED BY THE FUSION OF MUSIC AND FASHION IN WHAT BECAME KNOWN AS 'SWINGIN' LONDON'. ITS NERVE CENTRE WAS THE SOHO DISTRICT WHERE THE MARQUEE CLUB WAS BASED, AND NEARBY CARNABY STREET, WHERE MANY NEW SHOPS HAD OPENED TO SELL THE LATEST FASHIONS. THE MINISKIRT DESIGNED BY MARY QUANT, WAS A SYMBOL OF THE NEWLY-FOUND CONFIDENCE OF YOUNG WOMEN WHO WERE ENJOYING SEXUAL FREEDOM FOLLOWING THE INTRODUCTION OF RELIABLE CONTRACEPTION. QUANT, A DESIGNER OF WELSH ORIGIN, INVENTED A NEW LOOK FOR WOMEN TOO, VERY THIN WITH SHORT BOYISH HAIR, AS EMBODIED BY THE MODEL TWIGGY. SINGERS DUSTY SPRINGFIELD, SANDY SHAW, JULIE DRISCOLL AND CATHY MCGOWAN, THE PRESENTER OF THE SHOW *Ready Steady Go!* ALL BECAME STYLE ICONS FOR YOUNG WOMEN WHO REJECTED THE DEMURE FASHIONS OF THE 1950S IN FAVOUR OF A SLEEKER MORE ANDROGYNOUS LOOK.

Previous double page: Shimmering clothing for Pete Townshend, Roger Daltrey, John Entwistle and Keith Moon, who embody the Swingin' 60s in London. In 1968, The Who released the album *Magic Bus: The Who on Tour*.

Broadcasters exploited the populari-ty of the new music scene too with flagship TV shows like *Ready Steady Go!*, *Thank Your Lucky Stars* and *Top of the Pops* while pirate station Radio Caroline broke new ground and gained millions of listeners by broadcasting a wider range of music from a ship moored in international waters in the North Sea. Teenagers could tune in weekly to see the latest stars on TV such as the Beatles, with the release of their albums *Rubber Soul*, *Revolver* and *Sgt. Pepper's Lonely Hearts Club Band*, the Rolling Stones with *Aftermath* and *Their Satanic Majesties Request*, the Kinks with *Face to Face* or The Who with *A Quick One*.

New celebrities emerged like Marianne Faithfull, who recorded Jagger and Richards' 'As Tears Go By' and the Bee Gees, who, after leaving Australia to return to their native England in 1967, jostled the Beatles for top position in the charts thanks to the splendid melodies of 'New York Mining Disaster 1941', 'Massachusetts', or 'I Started a Joke'.

The Mods who appeared in the mid-1960s in London and in the seaside resorts of southern England, created their own alternative youth culture, distinct from the leather-clad rockers. As Pete Townshend of The Who wrote, "Mods were an expression of a rejection of everything that existed. They didn't want to know anything about what was being said on television, politics or the Vietnam war. If you were in a regular job, you weren't a Mod... To be a mod, you had to have short hair, money enough to buy a real smart suit, good shoes, good shirts; you had to be able to dance like a madman. You had to be in possession of plenty of pills all the time and always be pilled up. You had to have a scooter covered in lamps." Being a Mod was primarily a question of style and a new way of living (taking amphetamines to dance all night and projecting a sneering contempt for everything else). From a musical point of view, they were more at home with music of Black origin such as blues or ska rather than the blander pop music of the Hollies, for example. In addition to The Who's anthems, 'I Can't Explain', 'The Kids Are Alright', and especially 'My Generation', the Mods identified with the dandy look of the Kinks and especially with songs such as 'You Really Got Me', 'All Day And All Of The Night', 'Sunny Afternoon', and 'Dedicated Follower Of Fashion', a song in which the brilliant composer Ray Davies seriously mocks the shortcomings of Swingin' London.

Similarly, the Small Faces who, with 'Whatcha Gonna Do About It?', combined the anger of Black rhythm'n'blues with an English sensibility, or the Yardbirds (Jeff Beck era) and The Move who, with 'Shape Of Things' and 'Night Of Fear' respectively, established themselves in the annals of English rock during the 60s. But as the energy and confidence of the mid-60s subsided, so too English rock music would need to reinvent itself!

Left page and above: The Mod look of The Who. The Union Jack in the
background and on Pete Townshend's jacket, op art graphics for Keith Moon,
John Entwistle and Roger Daltrey. In 1965, The Who sang 'My Generation' and
their lyrics became a slogan: "I hope I die before I get old." Four years and
many hits later, they released the concept album *Tommy* – their major work.
Rock music was then at its zenith.
Next double page, from left to right: John Entwistle, Keith Moon,
Roger Daltrey and Pete Townshend.

Tom Jones in 1967. Comfortably seated on the hood of a Jaguar MK1, right
outside his home in Shepperton (near London), the singer enjoys his many
hits, starting with 'Green, Green Grass of Home' and 'What's New Pussycat?'
Right page: Tom Jones in the charming company of Sandy Shaw in 1966.
As fate would have it… the year before, Tom Jones had recorded 'It's Not
Unusual', a song originally intended for Sandy Shaw.

TOP OF T

By winning the Eurovision Song Contest 1967 with 'Puppet On A String', a hit she performed barefoot, Sandie Shaw became one of the most popular singers in the United Kingdom. At the time, London was home to a new female emancipation, marked by Mary Quant's miniskirt and the fashions of Carnaby Street. Sandie became a familiar face of the Swingin' 60s.

John Lennon, Ringo Starr, Paul McCartney and George Harrison promote ABC Television's flagship music show. The Beatles first appeared on *Thank Your Lucky Stars* on January 19, 1963 and performed 'Please Please Me', the first of several appearances on the show. Their last performance was on April 3, 1965. They played (in play-back) 'Eight Days A Week', 'Yes It Is', and 'Ticket To Ride'.
Next double page: The Beatles in their *Sgt. Pepper's Lonely Hearts Club Band* uniforms.

THE KINKS

Above: The Kinks helped create the spirit of Swingin' London with their sense of humour. The group was founded in 1963 in London. It includes (from left to right) Dave Davies, Peter Quaife, Mick Avory and Ray Davies and they would climb to the top of the rock hierarchy with songs such as 'You Really Got Me', 'Sunny Afternoon', and 'Waterloo Sunset'.
Right page: Ray Davies is the soul of the Kinks. A brilliant songwriter, he mocked the "slaves" of fashion in 'Dedicated Follower of Fashion'.

THE ROLLING STONES

Previous double page: The Rolling Stones pose for posterity in 1964, the year of their first American tour. The Edith Grove chapter, where Mick Jagger, Brian Jones and Keith Richards lived in their early days, is now a thing of the past. Above: Mick, Brian, Keith, Bill and Charlie in 1967. The year of many problems and scandals, but also the year of the huge successes of 'Let's Spend The Night Together' and 'Ruby Tuesday'.

Marianne Faithfull became known in 1964 for her version of the ballad 'As Tears Go By' by Mick Jagger and Keith Richards. Two years later, she and Mick Jagger would become one of the hottest media couples in town. It was not to last. With the Glimmer Twins, she also helped to create 'Sister Morphine'. Her version was released on disc two years before that of the Stones.

"Living with great artists like Ted Hughes or Mick Jagger is a very, very destructive position for a woman trying to be herself. In fact, it is impossible."

– MARIANNE FAITHFULL

Marianne Faithfull in 1967. Dressed by Daniel Hechter. That same year, the French fashion designer would go against the trends, while the miniskirt reigned everywhere in the West and especially in the streets of London, he produced a trump card with his long "maxi" skirts.

TWIGGY

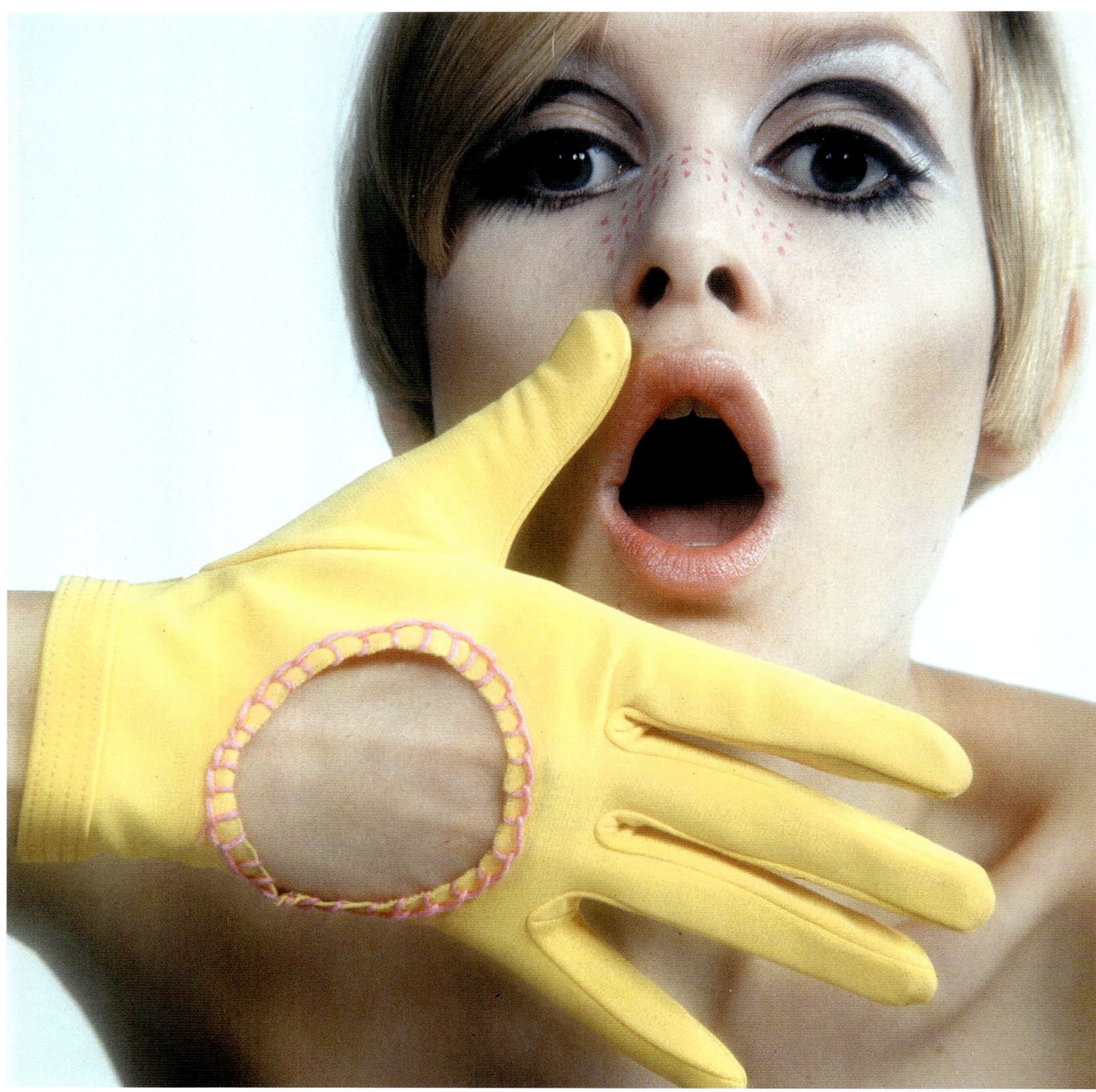

Previous double page and above: Twiggy "the twig" is to the fashion of
Swingin' London what the Beatles and the Rolling Stones are to music.
Discovered by photographer Barry Lategan, she epitomised an androgynous
look that ideally fitted the times and became a source of inspiration for the
queen of the 60s' fashion – Mary Quant herself. Twiggy graced the cover of all
the magazines, starting with *Vogue* and *Harper's Bazaar*. She eventually went
on to pursue a career as an actress.

Donovan is the troubadour from the foggy streets of Glasgow. He came to the fore in 1965 with 'Catch the Wind'. A unique singer-songwriter who followed his own path, mixing folk, rock, and psychedelia, a musical cocktail that he enriched with various exotic instruments. 'Sunshine Superman', 'Colours', 'Jennifer Juniper', 'Mellow Yellow'… folk romanticism in all its glory.
Above: Donovan pictured in his home in Maida Vale, London.

THE SMALL FACES

The Small Faces, Mod group par excellence, were one of the great revelations
of the year 1966 with 'All or Nothing' which is number 1 in England in August.
Two years later, they did a 180-degree turn by attempting psychedelic rock
with the concept album Ogdens' Nut Gone Flake.
Right page: The Small Faces photographed in 1966. From left to right: Steve
Marriott, Ronnie Lane, Ian McLaghan and Kenney Jones.

THE MOVE

Founded in Birmingham in December 1965, The Move had their first success
at the Marquee in London a few months later. In 1967, 'Night of Fear'
was released, reaching number 2 in the UK charts – a song received as an
anthem by the Mods. The Move is also one of the essential bedrocks of the
psychedelic scene.
Above, from left to right: Ace Kefford, Bev Bevan, Trevor Burton, Carl Wayne
and Roy Wood.

Cathy McGowan was the regular presenter of *Ready, Steady Go!* until the last program was broadcast in December 1966. Her influence was considerable, to the point that she was nicknamed the "queen of the Mods"...
"By the end of *Ready, Steady Go!* (thanks to Cathy McGowan), young people knew what they were going to listen to and what clothes to wear for the week ahead," writes journalist John Pratt.

Left page: Cream, which was founded in 1966, is the first supergroup in history. Their music, based on the blues, evolved into psychedelic rock and hard rock. Along with *Strange Brew, Sunshine of Your Love,* and *Tales of Brave Ulysses,* their album *Disraeli Gears* was a truly revolutionary work artistically.
Above, from left to right: drummer Ginger Baker, guitarist and vocalist Eric Clapton and bassist-vocalist Jack Bruce.
Next double page: Ginger Baker, Eric Clapton and Jack Bruce in 1966.

CYPR
£106
PIC

PETULA CLARK

When the French public discovered her in 1963 with Serge Gainsbourg's 'Vilaine fille mauvais garçon', Petula Clark already had a long career behind her in England. Her debut dates back to the dark hours of the Second World War when she sang on the BBC and was nicknamed the 'Singing Sweetheart'. Twenty years later, Petula became one of the stars of the 60s with 'Downtown', which shot to number 2 in the United Kingdom in November 1964, then sold three million copies in America the following year.

After the promising 'Matthew And Son' in 1967, Cat Stevens came back in force in 1970 with two notable albums, *Mona Bone Jakon* and *Tea For The Tillerman*. 'Lady D'Arbanville', 'Wild World', and 'Sad Lisa', among other songs, are the work of a songwriter of great sensitivity. After *Tea For The Tillerman*, *Teaser And The Firecat* (1971) was certified triple platinum in the United States.

Dusty Springfield is another triumphant symbol of the 60s in London, arguably the most talented blue-eyed soul singer with a string of hits that has toured the world, from 'I Only Want to Be with You' to 'Son of a Preacher Man' to 'You Don't Have To Say You Love Me'. Dusty Springfield also performed 'The Look of Love', the theme song for the James Bond film *Casino Royale* (1967).

Coming from Manchester, the Hollies emerged on the scene in 1963. 'I'm Alive', 'I Can't Let Go', 'Bus Stop', and 'Stop Stop' climbed to the top of the charts in 1965 and 1966, allowing comparison with the Beatles. Subtle melodies and careful arrangements were the keys to their success.
Above: The Hollies in 1968. From left to right: Graham Nash, Bernie Calvert, Bobby Elliott, Tony Hicks and Allan Clarke.
Left page: Graham Nash in 1970. The former Hollies' singer left England for California. He had a second wind with David Crosby, Stephen Stills and then with Neil Young.

THE BEE GEES

Before disco fever saw them fuelling the dancefloors, the Bee Gees chiselled
out some pure nuggets of 60s pop, including 'New York Mining Disaster 1941',
'Holiday', 'To Love Somebody', 'World', and 'Massachusetts', all released in 1967.
Above: The original line-up in 1967 includes (from left to right) Vince Melouney,
Maurice Gibb, Barry Gibb, Colin Peterson and Robin Gibb.

Top: Like the Hollies, Herman's Hermits hailed from Manchester and, like the Hollies, they became one of the major bands in beat music. 'I'm Into Something Good' reached number 1 in England in 1964. But it was with 'No Milk Today', two years later, that the band became known worldwide. Above, from left to right: Keith Hopwood, Derek Leckenby, Peter Noone, Barry Whitwam and Karl Green.

The Dave Clark Five can boast that they knocked the Beatles' 'I Want To Hold Your Hand' off the top of the charts in January 1964 and were the second British Invasion band (after the Beatles) to appear on the *Ed Sullivan Show*. Their hit song is titled 'Glad All Over'.

Above: Mike Smith, Lenny Davidson, Dave Clark, Rick Huxley and Denis Payton pose for the cover of their single 'Catch Us If You Can'. A feature film (by John Boorman) with the same title was made to promote the band and their songs

GUITAR HEROES

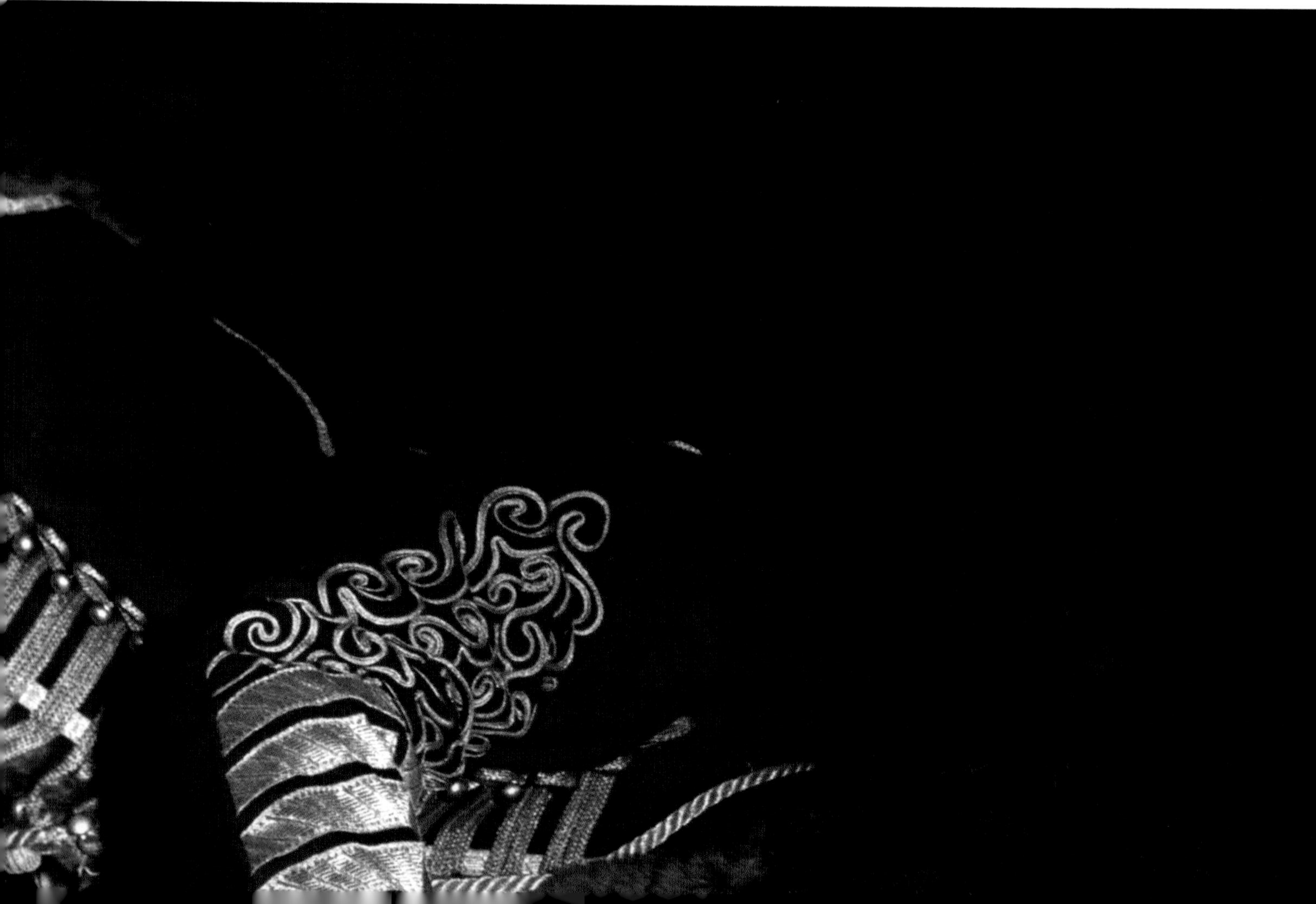

06.

GUITAR HEROES

SINCE A YOUNG DRIVER FROM MEMPHIS, TENNESSEE, NAMED ELVIS PRESLEY HAD THE GOOD IDEA, TO RECORD 'That's All Right (Mama)' WITH GUITARIST SCOTTY MOORE (AND BILL BLACK ON DOUBLE BASS), IN JULY 1954, THE ELECTRIC GUITAR HAS BEEN ELEVATED TO THE RANK OF SUPREME INSTRUMENT OF ROCK 'N' ROLL. SOME TEN YEARS LATER, THE GUITAR WOULD STILL BE THE MAIN DETONATOR OF THE BRITISH BEAT EXPLOSION. IT WAS HANK MARVIN OF THE SHADOWS WHO KICKED THE BALL OFF. AFTER HIM, GEORGE HARRISON PLAYED A RESTRAINED LEAD GUITAR, TO FIT PERFECTLY WITH THE POP MELODIES FORGED BY LENNON AND MCCARTNEY. AS FOR KEITH RICHARDS OF THE ROLLING STONES, HE ESTABLISHED HIMSELF WITH '(I Can't Get No) Satisfaction' IN 1965 AS THE ABSOLUTE MASTER OF THE GUTSY RIFF.

Double previous page: Jimi Hendrix and Eric Clapton at the Speakeasy in London in March 1967. The two greatest guitar heroes of rock in the 1960s have the blues as their first source of inspiration...

The Yardbirds, for their part, have the unique status of launcing three authentic guitar heroes. Eric Clapton, completed Keith Relf's line-up, then joined John Mayall's Blues-breakers in 1965 to stay close to the roots of English rhythm'n'blues. The following year, he took another decisive step by founding with Jack Bruce (bass) and Ginger Baker (drums) the legendary trio, Cream, the first supergroup in the history of rock. The result was several key albums, including *Disraeli Gears* (1967) and *Wheels Of Fire* (1968). Subsequently, Eric Clapton played in Blind Faith, then Delaney and Bonnie, before starting a solo career.

Jeff Beck succeeded Eric Clapton in the Yardbirds (at the suggestion of Jimmy Page) – the perfect opportunity for him to take his guitar-playing to the next level. In 1967, he left the Yardbirds and formed the Jeff Beck Group, which recorded *Truth* (1968) and *Beck-Ola* (1969), before creating a power trio with Tom Bogert (bass) and Carmine Appice (drums). He then inaugurated a solo career, notably marked by the jazz-rock album *Blow by Blow* (1975).

In 1968, Jimmy Page only played in the Yardbirds with Jeff Beck for a few months, before he went on to co-found Led Zeppelin with Robert Plant, John Paul Jones and John Bonham – one of the major bands in the history of rock, and an extraordinary laboratory of ideas, partly down to the exceptional virtuosity of the guitarist.

Other great British guitar heroes of the 1960s and 1970s, who should be mentioned, include Ritchie Blackmore of Deep Purple and Brian May of Queen. However, they were all developing their talent, their genius sometimes in the shadow of the greatest guitarist in rock history – the legendary – Jimi Hendrix.

Although Hendrix was born in Seattle, USA, it was in London, with the backing of his manager (and former member of The Animals, Chas Chandler), that he founded the Jimi Hendrix Experience with Noel Redding and Mitch Mitchell. This led to the singles 'Hey Joe', 'Purple Haze', and 'The Wind Cries Mary' in 1967, followed by the albums *Are You Experienced* and *Axis: Bold As Love*, also released in 1967, and *Electric Ladyland*, in 1968. Three albums that would become legendary in the course of rock history. It's impossible to assess the impact they had in the 60s and 70s, and their influence is felt even today!

Left page: Eric Clapton with his girlfriend, French model Charlotte Martin.
Within Cream, the so-called "God" Eric Clapton developed the language of the rock guitar.
Above: Eric Clapton adopted the afro hairstyle as a tribute to... Jimi Hendrix.

RITCHIE BLACKMORE

Ritchie Blackmore backstage. The lead guitarist of Deep Purple entered the very closed circle of virtuosos with songs such as 'Child in Time' and 'Highway Star' and with the riff (since copied a thousand times) of 'Smoke on the Water', he established himself as one of the first masters of hard rock. His instrument of choice is the Fender Stratocaster. One model even bears his name.

Jimmy Page was a studio musician and member of the Yardbirds before setting up
Led Zeppelin, destined to become one of the most influential bands in rock history.
He is an outstanding player on both electric guitar and acoustic guitar.
Next double page: Jimmy Page and John Bonham, respectively guitarist and drummer
of Led Zeppelin, play the dulcimer and flute on the banks of the Thames. A bucolic
image that corresponds to the spirit of the album *Led Zeppelin III*.

JEFF BECK

Jeff Beck also played for the Yardbirds before forming the Jeff Beck Group with Rod Stewart (vocals), Nicky Hopkins (piano), Ronnie Wood (bass) and Mick Waller (drums). Released in 1968, the album *Truth* is now considered one of the first testaments to heavy metal.
Right page: Jeff Beck guest of the television show *Midnight Special* in May 1975.

"Jimi Hendrix was making love to the stars," said his friend Eric Burdon. With his first singles, including 'Purple Haze', and the albums *Are You Experienced*, *Axis: Bold As Love*, and *Electric Ladyland*, the guitarist expanded the boundaries of rock like no one before him.

"When the power
of love overcomes
the love of power,
the world will know
peace."

– JIMI HENDRIX

Left page: Jimi Hendrix and his two English musicians from the Experience, drummer Mitch Mitchell (left) and bassist Noel Redding.
Above: Jimi Hendrix in the kitchen of his London apartment in 1967, the same year that he developed rock guitar with 'Foxy Lady', 'Third Stone From the Sun', and the ballad 'Little Wing'.
Next double page: Jimi Hendrix in 1968. His performance at the Monterey Festival a few months earlier had earned him new guitar hero stripes.

ALVIN LEE

Above: Guitarist Alvin Lee, pictured in front of Hook End Manor, the stunning mansion he bought near Checkendon, Oxfordshire. It was there, too, that he built the Space Studios. The leader of Ten Years After is the guitarist who plays faster than his shadow. He demonstrated this brilliantly at the Woodstock festival.
Right page: Ten Years After in an unguarded moment. From left to right: Chick Churchill, Alvin Lee, Ric Lee and Leo Lyons.

CREPES
SANDWICHES
TOAST
PIZZA
QUICHES
HOT DOG
SANDWICHES
BEUR
CREPES

07.

PROGRESSIVE ROCK

THE BEATLES GROUND-BREAKING ALBUM *Sergeant Pepper's Lonely Hearts Club Band* (1967) LED THE CHARGE. GRADUALLY, THE NEW BANDS WHICH BECAME KNOWN UNDER THE LABEL OF PROGRESSIVE ROCK, FREED THEMSELVES FROM THE INFLUENCE OF THE BLUES AND RHYTHM'N'BLUES AND INTRODUCED INTO THEIR MUSICAL COMPOSITIONS A WIDER RANGE OF INSTRUMENTS, SUCH AS THE FIRST SYNTHESIZERS, THE FLUTE AND SAXOPHONES. ALONGSIDE THE BEATLES, THE MOODY BLUES (*Days Of Future Passed*, 1967), PROCOL HARUM (*A Whiter Shade Of Pale,* 1967 ; *Grand Hotel*, 1973), KING CRIMSON (*In The Court*, 1969 ; *Larks' Tongues In Aspic*, 1973), EMERSON, LAKE & PALMER (*Tarkus*, 1971) AND YES (*Fragile*, 1971, *Close To The Edge*, 1972) CONSIDERABLY BROADENED THE HORIZON OF ROCK, SOMETIMES LAYING CLAIM TO THE HERITAGE OF THE GREAT COMPOSERS OF EUROPEAN TRADITION, FROM BACH TO DVORÁK, VIA MOZART, BEETHOVEN AND DEBUSSY.

Previous double page: Snacks and refreshment for the members of Genesis (post Peter Gabriel). From left to right: Tony Banks, Mike Rutherford, American session drummer Chester Thompson, Steve Hackett and Phil Collins.

While drawing on the classical music of the 17th and 18th centuries (such as Henry Purcell and Jean-Sébastien Bach), Jethro Tull drew equal inspiration from the English folk tradition for their albums *Benefit*, 1970; *Aqualung*, 1971. This is also the case for Genesis, whose development of multimedia stage acts combined with a symphonic music that plunges the listener into the heart of ancestral English legends and children's tales with *Trespass* (1969), *Nursery Cryme* (1971) *Foxtrot* (1972) and *Selling England by the Pound* (1973) – until *The Lamb Lies Down on Broadway* (1974) and the departure of Peter Gabriel.

The British progressive rock scene is intimately linked to the underground movement, notably the concert organised at the Roundhouse in Chalk Farm (London) for the launch of the *International Times* (IT) newspaper in October 1966, and the happenings organised at the Marquee in London, also in 1966, and known as the "Spontaneous Underground".

Pink Floyd and Soft Machine are two bands which intrinsically represent the amazing creative turbulence that England experienced in the second half of the 1960s. After exploring psychedelia with Syd Barrett (*The Piper at the Gates of Dawn*, 1967), Pink Floyd, with David Gilmour, created soaring, cosmic and melodic music that reached new heights with *Atom Heart Mother* (1970), *Meddle* (1971), *The Dark Side of the Moon* (1973) and *Wish You Were Here* (1975).

Failing to reach as wide an audience as that of Pink Floyd, Soft Machine is nevertheless a pillar of the English progressive rock movement. It is the leading group of the "Canterbury School", sounding like the synthesis of all countercultures, both European and American, with a fusion of the surrealist spirit of André Breton, the derision of the Dadaists, and the libertarian writing of the American poets of the Beat Generation (The name "Soft Machine" being derived from William Burroughs' novel *The Soft Machine*.) and the ideals of hippie philosophy. Musically, Soft Machine, originally featuring Kevin Ayers (vocals, guitar) and Robert Wyatt (vocals, drums), was heavily influenced by the modern jazz of Charlie Parker and John Coltrane, resulting in superb albums, such as *The Soft Machine* (1968) and *Third* (1970).

Kate Bush is another performer whose stage act and soprano singing were hard to classify. The first female singer-songwriter to have a number 1 hit with 'Wuthering Heights', her debut album *A Kick Inside* (1978) sold over a million copies. In 2022, a new generation of fans have rediscovered Bush through her song 'Running Up That Hill (A Deal with God)' (1985), which was a key element in the story for the fourth series of the Netflix hit *Stranger Things*.

THE MOODY BLUES

The Moody Blues, originally from Birmingham, are among the first British bands
to have been inspired by the music of European tradition. The album that breaks
with the American influence is entitled *Days Of Future Passed* and includes at its
end 'The Night: Nights in White Satin.'
Above: The Moody Blues in 1971. From left to right: Ray Thomas, Graeme Edge,
John Lodge, Mike Pinder and Justin Hayward.

**Mike Harrison is one of the very best singers in the progressive scene. He is well known
as the leader of the band Spooky Tooth, with whom he recorded *Ceremony* in 1969 in
collaboration with French composer Pierre Henry, and then, in 1970,
the album *The Last Puff* (which includes an unmissable version of The Beatles'
'I Am The Walrus'). He also had a solo career crowned with excellent albums,
including *Mike Harrison* in 1971.**

Soft Machine, which takes its name from a novel by William Burroughs, is the iconic band of the Canterbury school, a meeting between psychedelic rock, avant-garde and beat culture.
Above: The Canterbury formation in 1967. From left to right: Daevid Allen, Mike Ratledge, Robert Wyatt and Kevin Ayers.
Left page: Soft Machine with Hugh Hopper alongside Robert Wyatt and Mike Ratledge.

**Since the compositions 'In The Court' and '21st Century Schizoid Man' on the album
The Court Of The Crimson King in 1969, King Crimson have occupied a prominent
place on the British progressive rock scene, many thanks to the extraordinary
creativity of guitarist Robert Fripp (above).
Opposite page: King Crimson in the late 1970s. Robert Fripp is surrounded by Adrian
Belew, Bill Bruford and Tony Levin.**

Pink Floyd's career is exceptional. Coming from the London underground, the band rose to the top of the psychedelic movement with *The Piper at the Gates of Dawn* (1967), and then broke through to the top with soaring, symphonic music. Pink Floyd established itself as the definitive album of progressive rock with *The Dark Side of the Moon* in 1973. Opposite page, from left to right: Syd Barrett, Nick Mason, Rick Wright and Roger Waters. Above and next double page: Pink Floyd with David Gilmour (centre), successor to Syd Barrett.

4
HAY'S MEWS
4

MIKE OLDFIELD

Mike Oldfield became famous overnight in 1973 thanks to *Tubular Bells,* his first album and the first 33 rpm released on Virgin Records – a symphony fusing folk and progressive rock, whose piano introduction would serve as the theme tune for William Friedkin's film *The Exorcist* (1973). The brilliant composer continued on this path with *Hergest Ridge* (1974) and *Ommadawn* (1975).

Family was a major band of the British progressive rock scene. Their music was
built on the encounters of psychedelic rock, folk and jazz. In 1968, their first album,
Music in a Doll's House, was recorded in quintet: Roger Chapman, John "Charlie"
Whitney, Jim King, Ric Grech and Rob Townsend.
Above: Roger Chapman (right) with Jim Cregan who joined Family in 1972, before
the sessions of the last opus, *It's Only a Movie* (1973).

ELP

**Above: A virtuoso on piano and Hammond organ, and connoisseur of
classical music, Keith Emerson formed The Nice in 1967 with guitarist David
O'List. With psychedelic rock, baroque music, and covers of Dylan songs,
The Nice was innovative. But it was with Greg Lake and Carl Palmer that
Keith Emerson really turned progressive rock upside down. Emerson, Lake &
Palmer (ELP) sold some 40 million albums, including *Tarkus* (1971).
Page opposite, from left to right: Keith Emerson, Greg Lake and Carl Palmer.**

Originally a rhythm'n'blues band, Jethro Tull then turned to progressive rock. They mixed folk, rock and baroque music, giving a central place to Ian Anderson's flute, becoming one of the most original bands of the 1970s.
Above, from left to right: David Palmer and Clive Bunker (seated) and Glenn Cornick and Ian Anderson (standing).

In the early 1970s, Jethro Tull was at the top of their game. In 1971, the band from Blackpool
recorded their fourth studio album, which is also their masterpiece: *Aqualung* is a concept
album about God and religion, which sold more than seven million copies worldwide. The
following year the band pulled another masterstroke with *Thick as a Brick*, which reached
number 1 in the United States.
Jethro Tull in 1971. From left to right: Martin Barre, Ian Anderson, Jeffrey Hammond-
Hammond, Clive Bunker and John Evan.

At the age of 19, Kate Bush was the first female singer-songwriter in the UK to have a number 1 hit. The single, which stayed at the top for a month, was 'Wuthering Heights' included on her debut million-selling album *A Kick Inside* (1978). In 2022 she had another number 1 hit with 'Running up that Hill…', due to the inclusion of the track in the fourth series of *Stranger Things* on Netflix. Like Bowie, Bush trained with Lindsay Kemp to bring a more theatrical approach to her performances, which involved dance, mime, and burlesque.

The image above was used on the cover of the *Live at Hammersmith Odeon* album (1994) which was a re-release of a video recording made of Bush's *The Tour of Life* (1979). For this tour, to enable free movement on stage, she developed a headset with a wireless microphone, the predecessor to today's miked headsets.

Performed by top instrumentalists, Yes' symphonic music scored with the public in the early 1970s with the albums *Fragile* (1971) and *Close to the Edge* (1972). Above: The line-up of Yes in 1974. From left to right: Steve Howe, Patrick Moraz, Jon Anderson, Chris Squire and Alan White.
Next double page: Yes, in their greatest era. From left to right: Rick Wakeman, Chris Squire, Steve Howe, Bill Bruford and Jon Anderson.

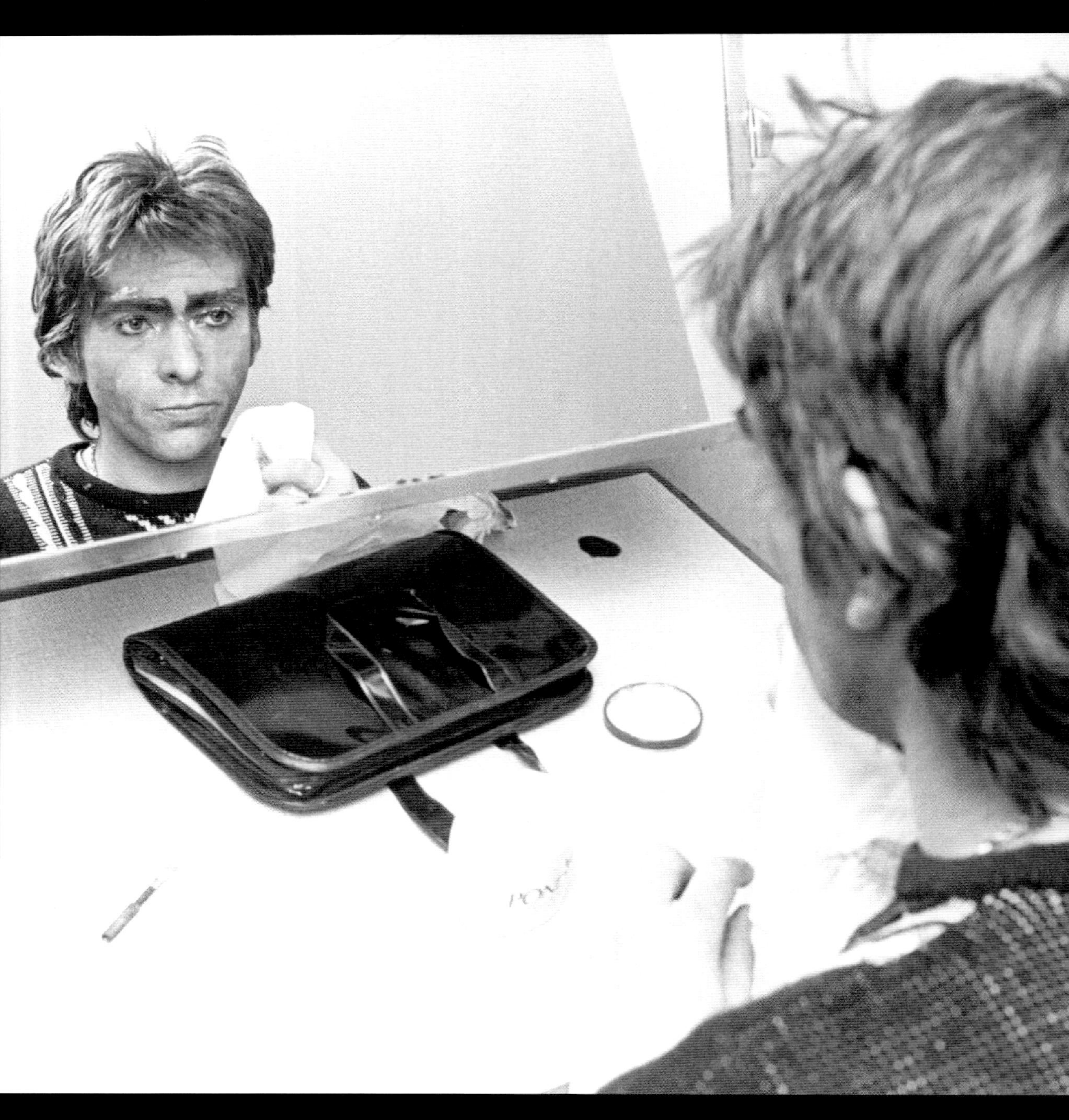

Peter Gabriel was the lead singer of Genesis from the band's debut in 1967 until the recording of the rock opera *The Lamb Lies Down on Broadway* in 1974.
Above: The singer in his dressing room during the performance of *The Lamb Lies Down on Broadway* in Copenhagen.
Right page: Genesis in the mid-1970s, after the departure of Peter Gabriel. From left to right: Phil Collins, Bill Bruford, Steve Hackett, Mike Rutherford and Tony Banks.
Next double page: The same line-up in Paris with a young fan.

RUE PARMENTIER
Vers Av ue du Roule

RUE PARMENTIER
Vers Levallois

With *Crime of the Century, Crisis? What Crisis?*, and *Breakfast in America*, released in 1974, 1975 and 1979 respectively, Supertramp contributed greatly to broadening the audience for progressive rock. Left page: Supertramp in 1977. From left to right: Bob Siebenberg, John Helliwell, Dougie Thomson, Roger Hodgson and Rick Davies.
Above: Supertramp in July 1970. From left to right: Rick Davies, Roger Hodgson, Richard Palmer-James, Robert Millar and Dave Winthrop.

08.

HEAVY METAL

IT WAS IN ENGLAND, AT THE END OF THE 1960S, THAT HEAVY METAL REALLY TOOK OFF. FORMED AFTER THE DISSOLUTION OF THE YARDBIRDS, LED ZEPPELIN APPEARED AS THE PROTOTYPE OF THIS NEW KIND OF HEAVY ROCK BAND. ITS LINE-UP FEATURED JIMMY PAGE, AN OUTSTANDING GUITARIST, ROBERT PLANT, A SEX SYMBOL SINGER, JOHN PAUL JONES, A BASSIST (AND KEYBOARDIST) OF GREAT INVENTIVENESS, AND JOHN BONHAM, A POWERFUL DRUMMER. IT IS FROM THIS ALCHEMY THAT LUMINOUS ALBUMS WERE CREATED: *LED ZEPPELIN I, II, III* AND *IV*, RELEASED BETWEEN 1969 AND 1971.

Previous double page: Hawkwind in 1974, pioneer band of 'space rock'.

Black Sabbath and Deep Purple are the two other cornerstones of English hard rock/heavy metal. Black Sabbath, composed of singer Ozzy Osbourne and guitarist Tony Iommi, rose to well-deserved fame with the album *Paranoid* (1970), which lodged at number one in the charts in England and the USA (and stayed there for more than a year). The Birmingham band sang about death, the devil, war and rebellion and their hypnotic riffs, combined with the macabre atmosphere of their stage act, created a frightening experience, which became known as "gothic" rock, a hybrid heavy rock genre.

After having ventured into the dangerous terrain of progressive rock (*Concerto for Group and Orchestra*, 1969), Deep Purple became one of the lynchpins of hard rock thanks to the single 'Black Night' and the album *Deep Purple in Rock* (1970), which was recorded with Ian Gillan (vocals), Ritchie Blackmore (guitar), Jon Lord (keyboards), Roger Glover (bass) and Ian Paice (drums). Soaring from Lord's classico-moderns, adding Blackmore's "pyrotechnic" guitar parts, Gillan's devastating voice and an infallible rhythm section, Deep Purple had found its style – a style that came to the zenith with *Machine Head* (1972) and anthems such as 'Smoke on the Water', 'Highway Star', 'Space Truckin'', and 'Lazy'.

In the early 1970s, in the wake of Led Zeppelin, Deep Purple and Black Sabbath, there was a calling for more heavy metal throughout the UK. Coming from the psychedelic scene, Status Quo moved from *Dog of Two Head* (1971) towards a kind of hard boogie dominated by the guitars of Mike Rossi and Richard Parfitt. Boogie with a hard rock sauce was also the preferred music style of Humble Pie and its guitarists Steve Marriott and Peter Frampton, as evidenced by the excellent *Rockin' At The Fillmore* (1971).

In a very different register, while mixing folk, progressive rock and hard rock, Uriah Heep, (whose name comes from a Dickens character), also gained success with the albums *Very 'eavy, Very 'umble* (1970) and *Look At Yourself* (1971). Other bands which trod similar heavy rock paths include Nazareth with *Razamanaz* (1973), Thin Lizzy with *Nightlife* (1974) and *Fighting* (1975), and even more with *Jailbreak* (and the hit 'The Boys Are Back in Town', 1976); three albums that allowed its leader Phil Lynott to show off his love of Hendrix. As for Hawkwind, in the late 1960s and again in the 1970s, when the band collaborated with science fiction writer Michael Moorcock, they forged a unique psychedelic and cosmic heavy metal sound heard to best effect on *In Search of Space* (1972), *Space Ritual* (1973) and *Warrior on the Edge Of Time* (1975).

Led Zeppelin took the lead in the hard rock/heavy metal movement in the late 1960s, and no band could catch up. Left page, from left to right: Robert Plant, Jimmy Page, John-Paul Jones and John Bonham (in the foreground).

Above: Led Zeppelin in 1969 at Château Marmont, a hotel on Sunset Boulevard, the favourite haunt for rock stars in Los Angeles.
Next double page: John-Paul Jones, his wife Maureen, their children and the family dog in 1970.

It was after being fired from Hawkwind that bassist Lemmy Kilmister founded Motörhead in 1975 with guitarist Larry Wallis and drummer Lucas Fox. A few years later, this time with "Fast" Eddie Clarke and Phil "Philty Animal" Taylor, success is at the rendezvous. *Overkill* (1979), *Bomber* (1979) and *Ace of Spades* (1980) are among the best of heavy metal.
Above: Motörhead in quartet. From left to right: Würzel, Phil Campbell, Lemmy Kilmister and Phil Taylor.

On the border of hard rock and heavy metal, Hawkwind also borrows a lot from the world of science fiction, especially that of Michael Moorcock, who participated in the recording of *Warrior on the Edge of Time* in 1975.
Hawkwind in 1973 (above). From left to right: Nik Turner, Dik Mik, Del Dettmar, Simon King, Dave Brock and Lemmy Kilmister.

BLACK SABBATH

It was with their second album, *Paranoid* in 1970 and the eponymous song, that a cult
began to be built in honour of Black Sabbath. A cult that rallied even more followers
with *Master of Reality* the following year, edging closer to gothic metal.
Above: Geezer Butler, Ozzy Osbourne, Tony Iommi and Bill Ward.
Right page: Black Sabbath in 1970.
Next double page: the four members of Black Sabbath, Bill Ward, Tony Iommi, Geezer
Butler and Ozzy Osbourne (from left to right).

NO S

Deep Purple was right to move away from symphonic rock to embrace the hard rock cause.
Deep Purple's *In Rock*, *Fireball* and especially *Machine Head*, released between 1970 and
1972, are the bedside albums of many hard rock addicts.
Above: Deep Purple Mark II. From left to right:
Roger Glover, Ian Gillan, Ian Paice, Jon Lord and Ritchie Blackmore.
Left page: Ian Gillan was the voice of Deep Purple during the band's golden years.

“Learning to
play with a big
amplifier is like
trying to control an
elephant.”

– RITCHIE BLACKMORE

Ritchie Blackmore, Ian Paice, Jon Lord, Roger Glover and Ian Gillan: the formation of the planetary consecration that entrusts to wax pure masterpieces of hard rock such as 'Child in Time' and 'Highway Star'. After the album *Who Do We Think We Are* in 1973, Deep Purple reached their third form, with the arrival of David Coverdale and Glenn Hughes in place of Ian Gillan and Roger Glover.
Next double page: Deep Purple Mark III, photographed at Clearwell Castle in Gloucestershire in September 1973. From left to right: Jon Lord, Ritchie Blackmore, David Coverdale, Glenn Hughes and Ian Paice.

PUB ROCK

09.

PUB ROCK

IN THE EARLY 1970S A NEW MUSICAL STREAM
APPEARED ON THE PUB CIRCUIT FOR BANDS
IN LONDON, SIMPLY CALLED 'PUB ROCK'.
IT WAS A GENRE THAT SAW A RETURN TO
THE ORIGINAL VIRTUES OF ROCK'N'ROLL
AND WAS A RADICAL REACTION AGAINST THE
"INTELLECTUAL DRIFT" AND GRAND SPECTACLE
OF THE PROGRESSIVE ROCK SCENE.
THESE BANDS REJECTED COSTUMES, CONCEPTS
AND LIGHT SHOWS IN FAVOUR OF UP-CLOSE
AUDIENCES AND SIMPLE BLUES ROCK
NUMBERS.
THEY WERE THE FORE-RUNNERS OF THE DIY
PUNK BANDS WHICH WOULD BURST ON TO THE
SCENE IN THE LATE 70S AND EARLY 80S.

Previous double page: Eddie and the Hot Rods, (or the Rods), a quartet from Essex best known for their 1977 UK top ten hit 'Do Anything You Wanna Do'. They had residencies at two pubs in London, The Nashville and The Kensington which led to a gig at The Marquee in 1977. Their support band that night was The Sex Pistols, playing their debut gig. It ended badly with The Pistols smashing up the Rods' instruments.

A regular fixture at the famous Islington pub, the Hope and Anchor, Brinsley Schwarz, a band named after their lead guitarist, preferred to take a simpler, less commercial approach to making music. They released two albums in 1970, *Brinsley Schwarz* and *Despite It All*. These revealed band member Nick Lowe as an extraordinary multi-instrumentalist.

At the forefront of Pub Rock, bands like Dr Feelgood, under the aegis of singer Lee Brilleaux and sneering guitarist Wilko Johnson, remade blues rock, with their seminal studio albums *Down by The Jetty* and *Malpractice* (1975), producing magical, high-energy performances, adored by audiences then and now. Their 1976 live album *Stupidity* reached number 1 in the album charts.

Ian Dury had formed Kilburn and the High Roads in 1971 and developed a fanbase on the Pub Rock circuit around London. Despite opening for The Who on tour in 1974, the group's record sales for albums *Handsome* (1975) and *Wotabunch!* (1978) never took off. Dury would go on to greater success with his band The Blockheads in 1977, and their single 'Sex & Drugs & Rock 'n' Roll' with its self-mocking lyrics, would chime with audiences tired of grand rock star antics.

Like Eddie and the Hotrods, The Stranglers were another band that started out on the London Pub Rock circuit and built a loyal following. With their angry lyrics and distinctive bass sound driven by JJ Burnel, they would later find fame in the Punk music scene with singles like 'No More Heroes' (1977) and 'Golden Brown' (1982).'

Due to the small audiences which Pub Rock bands attracted, they were mostly not on the radar of the major record labels so they began to write their own songs to home-record or work with small independent record labels. Lee Brilleaux helped his mates Jake Riviera and Dave Robinson to set up Stiff Records in 1976 and the label were the first to record The Damned and Elvis Costello, among others cutting their teeth on the circuit.

Pub Rock musicians went for an authentic 'live' sound, preferring to steer clear of studio effects and layering which they felt had squeezed the life out of rock music.

The Pub Rock circuit gave newer bands the opportunity to hone their skills in small venues. Other famous pubs on the circuit included the Tally Ho in Kentish Town, The Greyhound in Fulham, The Nashville in West Kensington and The Half Moon in Putney, a venue which is still offering live music to this day.

STAR SPORT
HIGGINS IN CAR DASH
It's no go for Wark
WHAT A WASTE!
McLean's move to protect managers
by JOHN MANN
WHO EARNS THE MOST IN BRITAIN?
FIND THE ANSWER ON PAGES 26-27

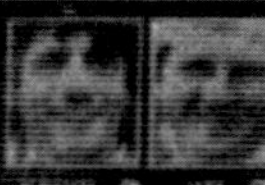

Dr. Feelgood returned to the basics of rock 'n' roll thanks to the pub circuit.
Above: The 1977 line-up includes (from left to right) Gypie Mayo, Lee Brilleaux, John B. Sparks
and John "The Big Figure" Martin.
Left page: Dr. Feelgood (early line-up) owes much of its success to Wilko Johnson and his
powerful rhythmic guitar playing.

JOE STRUMMER

In 1974, John Mellor aka Joe Strummer was playing rockabilly in a pub rock band called The 101ers, named for the Maida Vale squat he lived in. The group played on the pub rock circuit for a few years and had a residency at The Elgin pub in Notting Hill. In April 1976, the band were supported by The Sex Pistols at the Nashville and seeing the growing popularity of 'punk' music, just over a month later, Strummer decided to join another newly-formed 'punk' band who would call themselves The Clash. The Clash made their debut on 4 July 1976, supporting the Sex Pistols at the Black Swan in Sheffield.

"FOR EVERY GOOD SONG, I WRITE 20 BAD ONES
I HAVE TO CHUCK AWAY."
– IAN DURY

Ian Dury performing at the Roundhouse, Chalk Farm, in North London, 1978. By then, he had moved on
from Kilburn and the High Roads and formed his band Ian Dury and The Blockheads.
They had a hit song with 'Sex & Drugs & Rock 'n' Roll' (1977), recorded on the Stiff Records label.
Dury was an art teacher in his day job and had studied art at the Royal College of Art under Peter Blake,
the artist who designed the The Beatles' *Sgt. Pepper's Lonely Hearts Club Band* album cover (1967)

Alongside Dr. Feelgood, Brinsley Schwarz is the second pillar on which the pub rock scene was built. The first album (homonymous) was a nice test drive in 1970.
Above: Brinsley Schwarz in 1974. From left to right: Bob Andrews, Nick Lowe, Ian Gomm, Brinsley Schwarz and Billy Rankin.
Left page: Nick Lowe is the bassist and guitarist of Brinsley Schwarz. In 1975, he continued on his own to associate his name with the new generation of punk bands embodied by the Damned and Elvis Costello.

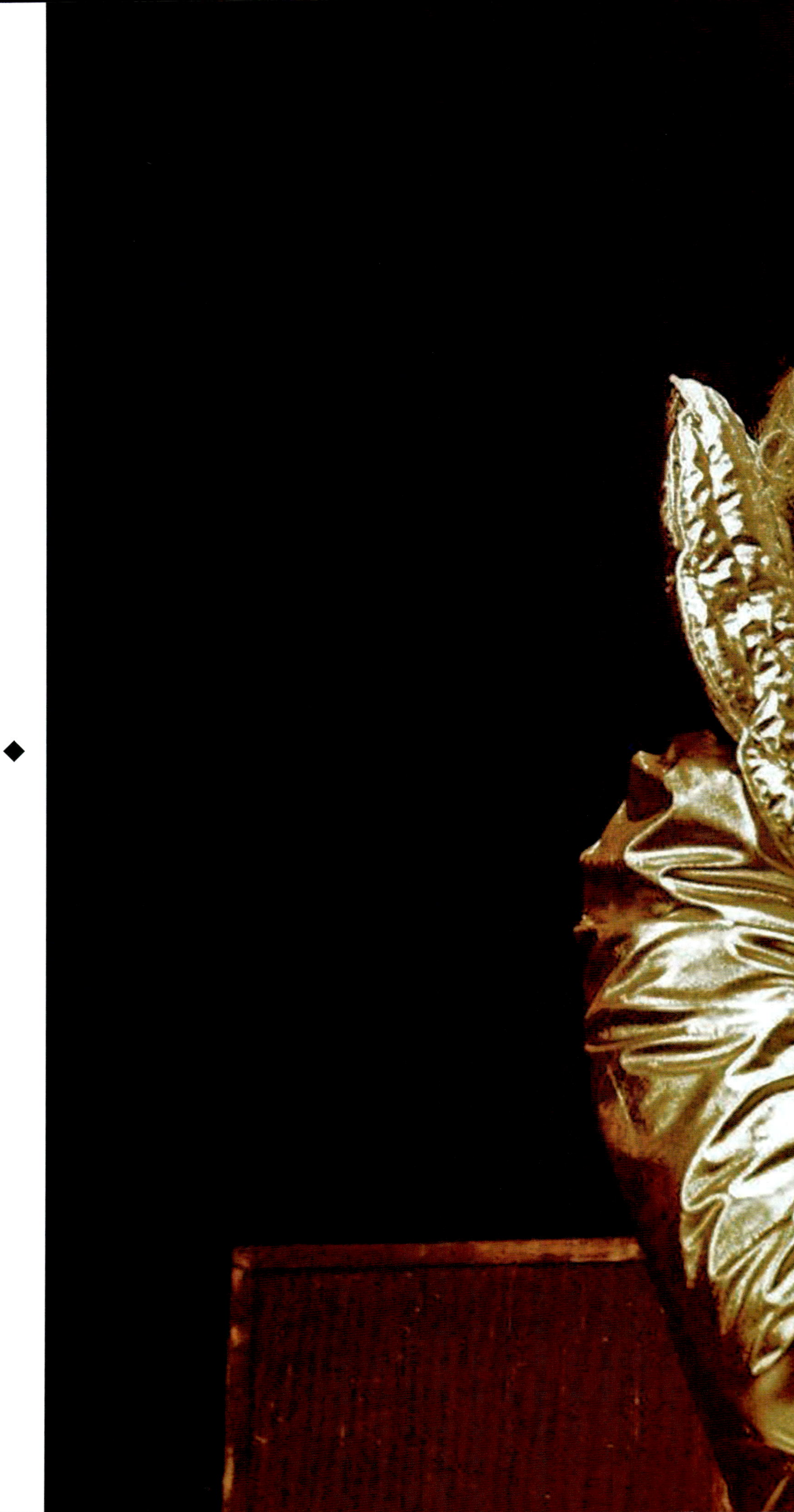

10.

GLAM ROCK

WITH MUSICIANS DONNING MAKE-UP, SEQUINS AND SPANGLES, PLATFORM-BOOTS AND LAMÉ JACKETS, GLAM ROCK APPEARED TO BRITISH TEENAGERS AS A WELCOME, MORE FUN ALTERNATIVE TO THE LOFTY HEIGHTS OF PROGRESSIVE ROCK. THE IRONY IS THAT IT WAS A FORMER MOD, ACCUSTOMED TO PLAYING IN THE UNDERGROUND CLUBS OF SOHO, WHO BECAME THE LEADING LIGHT OF THIS NEW GLAM ROCK SUB-CULTURE. HIS NAME WAS MARC FELD. RENAMED MARC BOLAN, THE YOUNG SINGER AND GUITARIST WITH CURLY HAIR, SHORTENED HIS BAND'S NAME FROM TYRANNOSAURUS REX TO T. REX, AND ENJOYED HUGE POPULARITY WITH THE HITS 'Ride a White Swan', 'Hot Love' AND 'Get It On' FROM THE AL-BUM *Electric Warrior* (1971).
FREDDIE MERCURY AND HIS BAND QUEEN SOON TOOK UP THE BATON WHERE BOLAN LEFT OFF… AND ELTON JOHN JOINED IN WITH EVER MORE FLAMBOYANT COSTUMES!

Previous page: Elton John in his glam rock phase performing in Hawaii, 1974.

Slade learned a lot from T. Rex and produced a string of catchy teen anthems such as 'Get Down and Get With It', 'Coz I Luv You', or 'Gudbuy T' Jane' (1973-74). They racked up more hits than any other band in the 1970s, selling more than fifty million albums worldwide and were one of the bands which developed a largely working-class fan base.

The pioneering female rocker Suzi Quatro broke through as a musician and bandleader during the 1970s. Supporting Slade and Thin Lizzy on tour in 1972, she released 'Can the Can' in 1973, which proved a number 1 hit in Europe and Australia. Managed by Mickie Most she had several hits including '48 Crash', 'Daytona Demon', 'The Wild One', and 'Your Mama Won't Like Me'. In the USA, she was better known for her role as bass player Leather Tuscadero in the sitcom *Happy Days*.

Paul Gadd jumped on the bandwagon of glam rock too. Taking the name Gary Glitter his hits include 'Rock And Roll (Part One)', 'Hello, Hello, I'm Back Again', and 'I'm The Leader Of The Gang (I Am!)' (1973-74) He would later fall from grace, convicted of numerous sex crimes, in 1999, 2006, and 2015 in the UK.

Another contender for glam rock fame is the band Sweet, who topped the charts in the mid-1970s with 'Hell Raiser', 'Ballroom Blitz' and 'Teenage Rampage'. Their songs were written by Nikky Chinn and Mike Chapman with catchy choruses and guitar riffs that guaranteed success.

Born David Jones, David Bowie used glam rock as a platform for his futuristic vision and style. Influenced by the Pretty Things, the Velvet Underground and Andy Warhol, his androgynous, decadent persona of Ziggy Stardust, stunned audiences and inspired teens. His amazing early albums display an artist telling stories and trying on characters for size. *Space Oddity* (1969), *The Man Who Sold the World* (1970) and *Hunky Dory* (1971) were well-received, but it was the concept album *The Rise and Fall of Ziggy Stardust and the Spiders from Mars* (1972), which captured the zeitgeist and earned a massive following.

Alongside David Bowie, art school graduates Bryan Ferry and Brian Eno came together in Roxy Music and took glam rock to a new level, seeking a fusion of music, modern art and fashion. Bryan Ferry, a miner's son from the North of England, adopted a suave persona as lead singer, which seemed to epitomise a new cool 'look' that had a very European feel. Brian Eno co-produced and played synthesiser on the first two albums before leaving to go solo.

Carving out a niche known as 'Art rock', Roxy Music's combination of art and style in their albums *Roxy Music* (1972), *For Your Pleasure* (1973), as well as those of *Stranded* (1973), *Country Life* (1974) and *Siren* (1975) inspired other bands to take control of their public image and musical direction.

When Tyrannosaurus Rex came out of underground clubs to become T. Rex, Marc
Bolan established himself as one of the great stars of the 70s.
Above: T. Rex's Marc Bolan (foreground) and his percussionist Mickey Finn.
Right page: T. Rex sparked the glam rock revolution in 1971 with the single 'Hot Love'
and the album *Electric Warrior*.
From left to right: Bill Legend, Marc Bolan, Mickey Finn and Stevie Currie.
Next double page: the same line-up in the same order.

It was not a large shift for Slade to move with their following in the skinhead movement and embrace the glam rock scene in the early 1970s. The band's songs are simple but terribly addictive when it comes to partying on Saturday nights. 'Coz I Luv You', 'Look Wot You Dun', and 'Cum on Feel the Noize' won the top places in the British charts, exerting influence on the Ramones and the Sex Pistols.
Right page, left to right: Dave Hill, Noddy Holder, Jim Lea and Don Powell.

QUEEN

The hearts of the four members of Queen swayed between glam rock and symphonic rock, at the beginning of their careers.
Above: Roger Taylor, Brian May, John Deacon and Freddie Mercury cross-dressed for the filming of the video to accompany 'I Want to Break Free' in 1984.
Right page: Freddie Mercury, a singer who was always able to convey emotion.
Next double page: Roger Taylor, Freddie Mercury, John Deacon and Brian May.

Above and the next page: Elton John connects to the glam movement for the extravagance
of his look. But this compulsive collector of pairs of glasses is first and foremost one of the
most brilliant melodists of English pop, ever since his *Tumbleweed Connection* in 1970.
Three years later, *Goodbye Yellow Brick Road* was released, which included three of his most
beautiful songs, 'Funeral for a Friend', 'Candle in the Wind', and 'Bennie and the Jets'. This
double album sold more than 30 million copies.

KIKI DEE

Kiki Dee began singing in a band in her home town of Bradford and was spotted in a talent contest. Her soulful voice garnered a contract with Tamla Motown Records in the USA – the first white singer from the UK to sign with the label.
Top photo above: Kiki with her band in Manchester in 1973, the year she signed with Elton John's Rocket label. The hits 'Amoureuse' (1973) and 'I've Got the Music in Me' (1974) followed, before her duet with Elton John (above) 'Don't Go Breaking My Heart' (1976) shot to number 1 on both the UK Singles Chart and the US Billboard Hot 100 chart.

Suzi Quatro was the first female rock musician to front her own band and play an instrument. Her glam rock look, powerful stance, and direct gaze influenced female acts to follow such as The Raincoats and paved the way for the Spice Girls and 'girlpower'. Her hits include 'Can the Can', '48 Crash', 'Daytona Demon', 'The Wild One', and 'Your Mama Won't Like Me'.

It is by marrying glamour and the avant-garde, with a touch of aristocratic elegance, that Roxy
Music brought an end to the hippie years and ushered in a new wave. From *Roxy Music* in 1972
to *Avalon* ten years later, their sophisticated blend of music has stood the test of time.
Above: Crooner, dandy, seducer, Bryan Ferry, the lead singer of Roxy Music.
Right page: Roxy Music glam version. In the foreground: Phil Manzanera; Brian Eno (left) and
Bryan Ferry (middle right) and Andy Mackay, John Porter and Paul Thompson (back).

**Founded in London in 1968, Sweet also contributed to the glam rock lustre
in the 1970s. In 1973 alone, 'Block Buster', 'Hell Raiser', and 'The Ballroom
Ritz' reached the highest levels of the British and other European charts.
From left to right: Brian Connolly, Andy Scott, Steve Priest and Mick Tucker.**

Between glam rock and soul, between pop and funk, Hot Chocolate found its style, which led it to the forefront of music news in the mid-1970s. Revealed with 'Love Is Life' in 1970, the London band triumphed with 'You Sexy Thing' in 1975, and then, two years later, with 'So You Win Again'. Moving from glam to disco, this has been the fate of Hot Chocolate. Above, from left to right: Patrick Olive, Larry Ferguson, Errol Brown and Harvey Hinsley; in the foreground: Tony Connor.

DAVID BOWIE

Above: David Bowie, nicknamed the "chameleon of rock". The rock star photographed in 1976. *Rebel Rebel*

"THE MINUTE YOU KNOW YOU'RE ON SAFE GROUND, YOU'RE DEAD."
–DAVID BOWIE

David Bowie may never have stopped challenging himself, but the glam period is nevertheless an essential part of his long career. Launched in 1972, *The Rise and Fall of Ziggy Stardust and the Spiders From Mars* is a major album in the history of rock.
Above: The androgynous image of David Bowie in his *The Man Who Sold the World* (1970) era.
Opposite page: The rock star with Angie Bowie and little Zowie.

BIBLIOGRAPHY

Colin Larkin, *The Guinness Who's Who of Seventies Music*, Guinness Publishing, 1993.
Bertrand Lemonnier, *L'Angleterre des Beatles*, Éditions Kimé, 1995.
Daniel Lesueur, *Hit Parades 1950-1998*, Alternatives et Parallèles, 1999.
Joel Whitburn, *The Billboard Book of Top 40 Hits*, Billboard Books, 2000.
British Hit Singles, *Guinness World Records*, 2001.
Shawn Levy, *Ready, Steady Go!*, Fourth Estate, 2002.
Mark Lewisohn, *The Complete Beatles Chronicle*, Hamlyn, 2006.
Barry Miles, *London Calling : A countercultural History of London since 1945*, Atlantic Books, 2010.
Jean-Michel Guesdon, Philippe Margotin, *Les Beatles, la totale*, Le Chêne/EPA, 2013.
Philippe Margotin, Jean-Michel Guesdon, *Les Rolling Stones, la totale*, Le Chêne/EPA, 2016.
Eds. R. Gillieron & C. Robson *Counterculture UK, a celebration*, Supernova Books, 2015.

PHOTO CREDITS

For more great books on music go to www.supernovabooks.co.uk